WHAT
HURTS
GOING
DOWN

BOOKS BY NANCY LEE

Dead Girls
The Age

WHAT
HURTS
GOING
DOWN

Poems

NANCY LEE

McClelland & Stewart

Library and Archives Canada Cataloguing in Publication

Title: What hurts going down / Nancy Lee.
Names: Lee, Nancy, 1970- author.
Description: Poems.
Identifiers: Canadiana (print) 20190162120 | Canadiana (ebook) 20190162201 |
ISBN 9780771049033 (softcover) | ISBN 9780771049040 (EPUB)
Classification: LCC PS8573.E34845 W53 2020 | DDC C811/.6—dc23

Published simultaneously in the United States of America by McClelland & Stewart, a division of Penguin Random House Canada Limited, a Penguin Random House Company

Library of Congress Control Number is available upon request

ISBN: 978-0-7710-4903-3
ebook ISBN: 978-0-7710-4904-0

Typeset in Legacy by M&S, Toronto
Book design: Emma Dolan
Cover image: © Number 1411 / Shutterstock
Printed and bound in Canada

McClelland & Stewart,
a division of Penguin Random House Canada Limited,
a Penguin Random House Company
www.penguinrandomhouse.ca

I 2 3 4 5   24 23 22 21 20

A note to the reader: poems in this book include depictions of sexual and physical violence.

CONTENTS

NO PLACE FOR A HEART

FOUR-EYED GIRLS

I'm sitting at the bar
with Mary Katherine Gallagher
watching prospects grind hope
into anything blond.

I've peeled off wool tights so
my pleated skirt flashes white
cotton panties when I cross
and uncross. No one notices.

For fun, we switch eyeglasses.
In hers, I drown. Fish wriggle
and shimmer, groove beyond
my reach. She says,

Through these glasses
everyone looks thinner. She says,
Why aren't there more girls
like us in movies? I tell her

there are plenty, floating
in rivers, folded in dumpsters,
naked, nameless. She says,
It's time for another shooter.

Something to clean the sink,
something the bartender
will set on fire, something
that hurts going down.

When Coco says, Are you kidding? to the filmmaker who shoots in the South of France like Godard, who tells her to loosen her blouse, already I know I will waste years auditioning for the part of girl-with-potential. A man wants to see how you take direction. Outside these rooms: parties, parking lots, corridors to empty elevators. After my first make-out session, the boy's best friend says, Next time, make her take her top off. Everyone's an auteur. Even Coco, shivering as she eases out of her shirt, hopes this film will be, if not art, then artsy. Maybe the next Antonioni is lurking in the frat house cellar, outside the gym bathroom, in a guest room piled with coats while his wife serves hot hors d'oeuvres downstairs. *Now take your thumb and put it in your mouth like a little schoolgirl.* Coco knows with the smell of old spunk and stale refrigerator, the cold against her nipples. Nobody goes to the South of France. Outside the door, a hallway of other doors, and behind each one, a man calling action.

The closest you have
to a nightmare is the dream
of feathers sprouting
from your tongue, the naked
bird-man frying bacon
in an iron skillet, pouring
jarred pennies over burnt
eggs. You wake gagging,
taste copper, clatter
of coins in your chest.

Nothing like TV
with flashbacks and court
dockets. No repressed
atrocities just memories made
worse with unremarkable
men. The gymnastics
coach who slipped
a finger into your leotard.
The painter in Peru
who took Polaroids
while your parents read
in his reception rooms, his oily
impression of you still hanging
in their breakfast nook.
The college boy
with a hump in his jeans
who trapped you in a Sunday
school bathroom, until

a mother with a stroller
pounded the door.

To admit this is to hurt
the ones you love. Blame
never goes where it should.
Your parents would succumb,
frail and foggy in plastic
bags of guilt. To keep them alive
you subscribe to silence, pay
dues in instalments at night.

*What is the number one cause
of pedophilia?* your date asks.
Sexy kids.
You laugh because you see it
in the candlelight on his neck,
the bristle of hidden feathers,
mark of a flock.

What movies of the week
never tell you is the difference
between knowing
and knowing. Only vultures
poke beaks into soft shells,
and still you dissect
the times you were called
precocious, still on bad days,
studying childhood
photos—a girl stands
in the grass in her mother's
hand-sewn rugby shorts
and looks sultry.

GIRL WITH BEAR

Basement den, electric fire, beer light
moon, bark walls. The boy buckles
and unbuckles, nods to AC/DC, ready
for what's his. Buzzed on gulps

of rum and Coke, she counts daylight
through chips in a painted window.
The bear skin prickles her feet, its tanned
edges stick to her heels. The boy says, *Get*

down. She kneels and kneads, expects
animal plush. The guard hair scratches.
He won it in a card game. Reeked
like a snatch until he had it cleaned.

She stretches to its paws, scabby
weights, picks at the nails. How long
before she can walk to Paul's Sub, sit
quiet in the greased air and eat? *Kiss it.*

She tries not to roll her eyes, opens
her mouth to the bear's neck: rain-sluiced
pollen, crusted grubs, cedar rot, an eddy
of salmon scales. *What does your dad do*

down here? Her fingers patter a snout's
proud jut, lip satin, teeth like horn
and rock. When the tongue rattles
stiff in her palm, she squeals, retreats.

Fuck, the boy says. He is different
in mirrored sunglasses. Drink empty,
belt wound 'round his fist. He is
as strong as his father. Close overhead

pine brush crackles. The bear rumbles
with dreams, roused by her wrists tied
near his mouth. Just a whiff of her
and he's arching, ready to bite down.

Start a fire with women's bodies; stack them deep for heat. What keeps a kind girl alive in the wild? The men in town are crapshoots, sawbucks, coins striking heads and tails. They post naked snaps of her on 4chan, ferry fifteen-year-olds across state lines, weigh options like: hands up her skirt, hands around her throat. She's ready for a chorus of frogs, a convent timeshare, ready to train a dildo to mow the lawn. Abandon romance. This one's for mothers who catch their boyfriends fingering their daughters. Here's to BFF date rape in the old man's sedan. Today a high school football coach showed cheerleaders the glory of his half-hard penis in a hot dog bun, tomorrow a man will cram his wife into a Naugahyde suitcase and drag her to the river. It's so fucking hot inside; she isn't surprised.

Record rainfall and ruin, grey water
under the sink, the landlord's grunting
messages, and ringworm: alien spores
glowing red in the creases of her skin.
The discount therapist charges fifty
an hour, so she talks fast, the Sally Ann
is out of winter coats, damp has left her
cardigan matted like a dog, she suspects
other students host dinners and exclude
her. The therapist's advice, slow down
and write, favours sentence-level
catharsis, the elixir of a finished degree.

Hydro is free, so it's hot baths and zinc
soap, itchy circles doubling in the steamed
mirror. In line at a food bank, she tries
to read past hunger. Tuesdays she pays
the shrink to talk, talk, talk. Loneliness
persists. She crashes a mid-term party,
summer dress under the dog sweater, forgets
to shave her legs, eats all the cheese, collects
hugs until someone notices her rash, until
she hears others have been to his boat.
Doesn't he do the greatest impression
of seven presidents? They knew nothing
of wine or writing before him.

She remembers his boat never leaving
the dock, his manuscript a centrepiece
on the dinette, but can't recall how he wrote
or how much tuition she'd paid to find out.
Doesn't know the names of dials or charts
and can't describe the nature of tides,
the tinny folk music playing from laptop
speakers or the change in his voice
when she tried to talk about her own book.
She can't explain why, without going to sea,
her legs jellied on the ramp or why the strap
of her shoe was so cheap it snapped
when his knee pinned her knee.

She leaves the party as people dance,
certain she'll lose the apartment, end up
calling home from a pay phone, rain
pooling in her garbage bags of clothes,
and empty notebooks. Her mother will cry
at the timing, the cost and trouble
of a last-minute flight. She'll promise
to repay, try harder at the next thing.
Drizzle will set a funk in her body,
the sweater so rank and spoiled by mildew,
she'll be forced to undress in the street.

In this story the cockroach is the man,
the curtain my girlhood, the creamed
corn spilled by the mother wasted
familial love, the father's zealotry
a metaphor for emotional blindness.

In this story the radioactive dinosaur
is the man, the city of Tokyo my body,
and the metro tunnel, well, you know.
Fire is fire. Explosions are explosions.
The snow-capped summit of Mount Fuji
signifies faith's chilly endurance.

A facet of the man is represented by
each of the three Magi in this story.
Do not accept his gifts. It's an honest
mistake to assume I'm the Baby
Jesus, but let's face it, I'm the slut,
Mary, whom no one believes
is a virgin, especially not the man.

Gothic romance man owns a mansion
with a special tap for instant boiling
water and acres of heated tile floor.
I'm the maid who scrubs the floor
and sometimes has her hand held
under the tap. The crazy woman
in the attic is me. The horse that won't
be broken is me. The intergenerational

family curse is me. The pig the man
whips for being pig-like is me.

In this story the man is the man
and I am me. His penis is his penis
and my mouth, my mouth. The bed
is my childhood bed, the guest room
bed, the bed in my college dorm
and the futon in my first apartment.
The parents watching TV are my parents,
and the thin scar on my thumb,
the thumb I am showing you now,
is where he sliced me with a razor
to prove he could open me at will.

ALPHAS

i.

At three a.m., lip gloss and crop tops
wasted in empty clubs, only you
are brave enough for new terrain.
We hunt at a crawl, every gin joint
gated, marquee dim. On the boulevard,
we roll down windows to watch
a coyote lope, head bowed. A bloody
rabbit swings from his jaw.
I tell you he's my first.

ii.

Alphas beside the car. Caps pulled,
track suits baggy, shoulders rolling,
chests sunk, a lazy jog with beer cans,
sidewalk be damned. The pack must
get hungry at three a.m. They stare
through glass, blow their liquored smoke.
I say, Ask where they're going.
You shake your head. The night
is wild with them.

iii.

Once, in a town on the coast you
chose celibacy over the hazard
of ocean men, woodsmen,
mountain men, unwashed hair
in pelts. Men with thick paws,
bark faces, who stank of wood chip,
coal dust, fish. When they entered
your bed tangled in nets and splinters
snuffled wet muzzles to your neck,
you played dead.

iv.

Now you raise two hatchlings
in a sanctuary. You pound fence posts,
lay tripwire, stock bear bangs, kneel
at the water to check muddy ground
for tracks. Satellites beam our hushed
talk of coyotes, mangy middle-aged
cheeks, half-eaten carcasses, how they
chew old wounds, cut and run.
We forget their feral cologne,
teeth and charm, until they startle us
from the stupor of married sleep.

The best was having nothing. No hope.
We wore what we wore: low-cut, tasselled,
pleathered, hitched up the thigh. We smacked
away comers, nails sharpened to pins.
They sucked wounds, called us bitches
but with a smile, the word stinking of aftershave
and jet fuel. We danced alone, a loose-hipped
shimmy, knees spread. Without hope
we were ascendant, effervescent, skinning
atmosphere. Terrestrials circled in ball caps
and jerseys, in Lacoste, in waxy black lambskin
scrunched to the elbows. We danced an orbit,
shoulders together, faces out, stared through
those men like space dust. Bitches.
After the club, we'd float in a wire capsule
fire escape, smoke clove cigarettes, sip warm
juice and vodka, free ankles from buckles.
The city winked below; men shrunk
to specks. We listened for sirens,
the call of girls preparing for liftoff.

January and I'm washed up in a silver bikini
at a bar by an off-ramp reading a man's dirty
palm. Ring of Solomon, girdle of Venus,

blister of oil and gas. His hips buck restless
under the table. Behind him, on a Lucite
stage, a girl in vinyl thigh-highs works

for her supper, hot pants peeled to a pale
lasered crescent, baby tee hitched over
baby breasts, ass lassoing a disco beat.

The boys at school crooned her name. Denim
and greasy hair. They had a way of bluing
the gravel path home, town lights hissing at dusk.

She lies naked on a quilt, legs twisting a tail.
The man throws crumpled bills on the table,
snatches them up, mutters, he only wants sex.

I blink and smile and count. And just like that
the future's coming; those boys, always
in the distance, no time to hold your breath.

In the cemetery, reeking
of Malibu and vomit, we crawled
over manicured turf, shuffled tarot,
shook runes, solved the arithmetic
of headstones, keened like widows,
wrists to foreheads, dry-humped
graves of lost men.

We lifted our skirts so dew
dampened the parts our panties
didn't touch, clasped hands to spirits:
Lucifer, Damien, Candyman.
And knowing nothing of the value
of souls, offered ours to damnation
for a real live husband.

> The boys who walked us home,
> Catholic and glad for any excuse
> to leave a party, waited stricken,
> murmured, *Don't. No really.*
> *Don't.* as we exhumed our Exorcist
> growls, our Jamie Lee screams,
> when speaking in tongues we
> writhed and mimed unzipping
> their warm polyester dress pants.

In the sequel, none of us finds peace
beside a husband. One blazes
with chemo then cools to ash in an urn

misplaced by an airline. One surrenders
a house and car to a weight-loss guru
with a sports betting G-spot and three
wives in Tulsa. One wastes years
haunting the internet for love,

then readies a feast alone
in the woods. Three shots of Malibu,
buried talismans: rabbit's foot, rosary,
runes. She cradles a knife, vigilant
for Freddie or Michael or Jason.
Dawn she will slash a path
through brush, swim naked
in lake weed, let it root in her
throat and hair.

That'll show her is how men say
goodbye. She opens her robe
and the lifeguard splutters,

the conductor bows, the realtor
measures every square inch,
the welder shields his eyes.

After, they hot-rod out of her drive,
she watches TV with a TV dinner, avoids
the bathroom mirror,

tired of what boils and bubbles
over, the excess of biology
texts and dirty magazines.

On the bus, briefcases stake seats
while she aches in heels. The bank clerk
who freezes her credit guffaws

when he can't get a date. At the grocer's,
men who won't pay bills or rake her leaves,
steer wives and kids as if she's a spill.

She tails them down aisles of cereal
and soup, says, sorry, sorry, sorry, her empty
cart banging their trousered hips blue.

HEN NIGHT

That night, after tiaras and shooters,
after the lubed grind of male strippers,
we prowled the streets sweating Chablis,
spotted that guy and shouted, Hey Baby,
we want to ask you something. Trailed him

through a gravel parking lot. Hair gel,
aftershave, Euro-fitted shirt—his primping
riled us. Hold up, Loverboy, don't be that way.
Flung a pebble to peck the back of his head.
When he ran, we ran. When he tripped,

we held him against a construction site
fence, our body glitter swirling in the yellow
security light. Shhh, we don't want to
hurt you. But by then, we did. Pushed
fingers past lips, twisted buttons from a shirt.

How many hands to hold a man steady,
how many women carry knives in a purse?
Back home babies slept. We slid into beds
beside husbands fitful with dreams of green
fees, tax havens, reno plans for the den.

There, there, we said, Don't worry
yourself sick. All the time tasting
that Axe-scented blood and heart,
smelling him on our feathers,
his swoon and our hungry clucks.

I

She wishes for a bandanna,
knotted tight to cover her eyes.
His gross joke about corncobs, truck rutting
an unpaved road. The kids in detention
will tell everyone

what they saw: miniskirt in November,
leaned against his cab in a push-up bra. Blame
Jean Naté and strawberry gloss. Under her thighs,
the rumbling city slips smooth.
Next stop highway,

forest, mountains. *Don't worry,*
I'll feed you. As if hunger's her problem.
He looked younger in the gym parking lot.
Sun, shade, sun. She squints
to remember his face.

When she's home she'll write
two lists in her diary, one about him: red
T-shirt, frayed sleeve, ginger stubble, gold stud;
another with all the things they'll say
she did wrong.

2

Pit stops she wears sunglasses,
hair bunched under a Jay's cap. She traces
shelves of candy, torn cardboard cradles, flips
stiff pages of swimsuit issues, watches
him watch her

through the station's barred
window; he holds the nozzle like a gun.
Behind her, an old man chuckles, *Your mother*
know you're reading that, son?
Pages of girls her age

surf-sprayed in deerskin and mesh,
bikinis of fine beaded glass. She turns
and smiles, ease on display, and the old man tips
his white Stetson, *Sorry, Miss,*
my mistake. She mouths,

Help, but the man just grins, distant
with embarrassment. *You like the fashions?*
Electric doors slur a chime, boots at the threshold.
Try again next week. *They take those girls*
to the ends of the earth.

3

Good days she dabs at mayo
in the corners of his mouth, chats
to the waitress about community college like she
take notes evenings and doesn't service
three rig pigs on payday.

At the mall she studies his staring.
Is he handsome? Life is lemons, her mother
would say. She worries her parents have gotten old.
Maybe if she returned with a fiancé
instead of in handcuffs.

Dumb luck and misunderstanding.
She's seen photos of girls who came before
and doesn't want to get hard, turn 'em out by the sink.
Some days she thinks about toilet cleaner
in his food, a lighter to the bed.

Then she remembers the petit point
roses of her mother's china, the tidy tools
in her father's shed, and knows they would cry to hear
such terrible schemes, to see her now,
a half-grown girl full of mistakes.

THE MOST GIRL PART OF YOU

ARRIVAL

In the splinters of ice watering
his third whisky, in the blinking
sequins of her half-price dress.

In the peach schnapps hot
on her gums, the cigar's bitter
rub in his cheek. In the rabble's

toasts and jokes, music jigging
their limbs, in the way all new
songs turn old. Skimming

cobbles in the tick tack
of heels, coiled around his tuneless
hum. In the boxspring's creak,

his coarse whisper, her quiet
prayer, back and forth.
Landing in emptiness

between his groan and cough,
I sully the stillness
of her heaviest sigh.

HUSBANDRY

My hands part a veil of flies.
Dogs in the gully are slow to rot,
rigored, insects rippling fur.
The gardener's devotion to our hens
slickens my heart, itches in the back
of my neck. Mongrels are no match
for his touch on a rifle.

A boy and I scrabble behind the rusted
oil tank, its belly hollow like the dogs.
We shade a magazine's glazed pages.
His nose drips a summer cold,
tongue pokes a lozenge.
He wheezes winter, eucalyptus.

The woman in the picture sits as I
sometimes sit in my dad's recliner,
leg hitched over the cushioned arm.
Behind her, trinkets clutter
a bookcase, a lamp drips pearls.
Her blouse gapes peachy breasts
that make me chew my lips.

The boy points to her sheered
pelt, ruffled flesh nestling;
even in a photo it trembles
like an animal just trained to heel.
That's what you're gonna look like.

How will I master her languid
disinterest, slung angles and bored
eyes? Already I can't swallow
without gurgling, and the pinprick
heat of the boy's shoulder dares
me to tumble him as he licks
a finger, unsticks the page.

To slow the pulse in my throat,
blot the sweat between my legs,
I think of how the woman must be
old: antique desk, folded glasses
on a chain, a fussy whorl
of scarves. She is not a girl

in cut-offs and flip-flops who
too often imagines the gardener's
shirt taut at the sight of a feral
bitch, easy hands loading
his gun, snapping the barrel
like a length of rope, fixing
to tie a wild dog in knots.

College girls by the pool table, flared
and feathered, shuffling darts, jukebox preaching
heartbreak and my dad propped at the bar, greased
knuckles, wallet empty.

Back at home, my mom
soaks car mags in lighter fluid, scores work shirts
with shears. Dinner cold, dishpan hands tight
for a night of tallying faults.

Later, when he hits her,
a reflection will stumble in the window, and she'll
gasp at the trespasser falling outside. So why rush
when I can slink

booth to booth,
down yeasty inches of beer, suck the lipsticked
tips of smoked cigarettes, sulk in my French cuts
and halter until I'm slumped

beside a man whose T-shirt
marshmallows over his belt, his ringed fingers
picking my denim pleats. When the bartender
shouts, *Who let*

the goddamned kid in? my dad
will turn, eyes leaking gin. Her torn pin curls
and bloody nose for six nights after girls titter
at the dartboard marking time.

> "The issue on this appeal is whether an infant model may disaffirm a prior
> unrestricted consent executed on her behalf by her parent and maintain an
> action pursuant to section 51 of the Civil Rights Law against her photographer
> for republication of photographs of her. We hold that she may not."
>
> —*Judge's ruling against Brooke Shields in her attempt to prevent
> further use of nude photos taken when she was ten years old.*

The problem of her appeal, larval
Mazola-sheened in a bathtub
of smoke, necklace heavy
as choke, rib ripple chest of a boy.
Camera hung between his legs,
the photographer grunts,

as if this is work.
A mother has ruined two pairs
of heels dragging a lazy girl
to castings; a lens need only wink
at rouged cheekbones and all
a child's body can't keep.

On the issue of breasts, the mother
is decided: drape them in white
eyelet and tulle, veil their puffy
lure, coral shadow, nude across
the lips, knee socks, school
books, loose, willing hair.

The photographer sighs.
The shower wand's black asp

scales the girl's hip, dribbles
down her arm. But she holds it
all wrong, as if it's a telephone,
as if there's someone to call.

MONTECITO

Evening calms the helicopters. Charred
juniper and shuttered houses. My soggy heap
of takeout containers, empty Fanta cans.

Franklin calls from Ho's Palace, says, *No
more delivery*, says, *Better call the Mister*,
means father: barefoot sunglassed purveyor

of single malt apologies and exotic pets,
lingering cigarillo smoke, a coolant stain
on the drive. For an hour late morning,

mother shuffles. *Fetch my pills*. Hauls
luggage, listens for men with megaphones,
then naps. Surely the aquarium will simmer.

I ladle fish into an ice bucket, run them
to the pool. The jewelled dead rise
so quickly. I swim with the bodies and cry.

Mother's lineless face nestled
in the buttery lapel of her beaver caplet,
stockings sagged as if she's shrinking.

I stroke her eyelids, smear wing dust,
steady a mirror to her lips, catch fog.
The sheets, her hair, dry enough to burn.

In the north, bombers cast banners
of neon dust. Our names on the news,
Toro, Montecito, Camino, flames melting

aluminum. Mother drowns necklaces
and silverware; pearls curl back to the sea,
our samovar a genie's lamp below

my kicking feet. When it hurts to breathe
I count inhalers in the cabana, reconsider
padlocked boxes in the garden's far

corner: rations, water, gas masks, flares.
To go there alone, to part the tall grasses,
to see the tiger cub in her cage,

huffing by a puddle of baby formula,
crusty-eyed, belly bloated, neck
limp in her diamond collar.

we are starved, sick with litany,
stomachs roughening against fathers,
secret ribbons in our hair.

Men consecrate lot lines
while daughters do the bed work
of wives. Come harvest,

we streak through bramble,
twig to twig, collect snakes in bonnets,
sip hen's blood and oracle futures

laced and sworn. In the river, we spit
his name into the mouths of brook trout,
tear their red bellies

and squeeze out spawn. We cast
him back to chapped arms, a girl
of twelve, raw from bucking

laundry beside his frozen wife.
A husband's gluttony is a sad pageant.
Stinking of horse sweat, he tore

her apron and fashioned a false
hero's coat from its threads. The pulpit's
rod chastens as its staff lifts

our skirts. How easily
witches are made. The doctor cuts
and all we do is bleed. We chant

for alchemy and iron bones
as gossip singes straw, ignites
the tinder of limbs.

DAUGHTERS

i.

Tell the daughters we were heartless,
crouched behind trees with rusted
wire. That flanks bucked as we bled
the bodies on beds of pine, stabbed
with flint blades and the ends
of spoons from a grandmother's
hope chest. Eyes whaled white, pupils
drained of ink. One by one in the fog
of morning, we scrubbed them
from our petticoats.

ii.

Stretched and sticky in the sourdough
starter, shovels scraping the stable
floor, scouring water in the tin tub,
sewing flecked with blood. A childhood
bridled, saddled, stung with lye, hung
to cure in salt and sun. No one
believed what their eyes didn't see,
what gnawed through a girl, rustled
her work-worn body in the brush.

iii.

Did they even want daughters?
Sons so adored, rut-hungry, bottle-weak,
sloppy work with a scythe. Who didn't
know his charm, the lanolin musk
of his wool? And what if all daughters
turned to ghosts? Whale bone, sadness,
smoke. Tell them, it was kill or be
killed. Tell them, we shivered for days
beside their cribs, then stood
to answer our own prayers.

PASTORAL

a quilt feather twisting in moted light
a panicked dog chained in the bed
of his truck radio squawking AM
the smell of fresh paint and turpentine
his saliva on the rim of my juice glass
the newspaper story of a man crushed
in a hippo's jaw and the farmer gobbled
by his own prized hog trampled
cornflowers outside my bedroom sill
the milk boiled down to burnt skin
in the pan a trick with a doll and three
pieces of string and a chair jammed
under a broken doorknob a branch forced
through an unoiled keyhole the preacher
on the dais in his satin-stitched stole saying
today thank your parents for punishing you
you who are filthiest with sin

Behind the back sink of the fourth floor girls' can.
Rosa kept the razor in a patchwork pencil case.
The metal handle's cold weight, solemn unscrewing

of the blade. We took turns, raised arms, etched tiny
Xs in the baby flesh of triceps, wadded paper
over blood. A spell against Jiffy Marker scrawls

that swore we were hot fucks, a hex for the boys
who barred gym doors unless we flashed our bras,
a pox on the cologned teacher who rubbed our backs

while checking homework. Xs stinging in the heat
of armpits, hardened to scabs we picked and peeled;
each day, new burdens, new crosses. We promised

to marry jobs, love test tube babies. Kept our hair
short, nails bare, wore the same bossy Oxfords,
and tried not to panic when we caught Philippa

laughing at Jimmy B.'s jokes in the cafeteria. Or Elaine
kissing Dan F. in the band room, clarinet in pieces
at her feet. Or Tracy with Roger T. by the Ancient

Worlds shelf in the library, her horn-rims cocked
sloppily, flaky hands up the front of her shirt.
Warm pipes, leaky sinks, chipped tile, our rituals

dwindled, until Rosa confessed she'd lost the razor,
pencil case ransacked by Mark W., who was taking her
to the movies on Saturday. Skins thickened. Hair grew.

Xs faded to rumour, faint ink in diaries, on divorce
papers, restraining orders. The lighter the mark,
the deeper the cut, and no one's blood to console us.

The gun tower is nothing but a cement bunker with a floor of broken glass. Rusted ladder, condom husks, beer cans, window sawed-out to the shore. She tries not to dwell on missing chemistry, Carla with her dagger pipette. *a searchlight, million candles* His cadet voice loud then lost like a badly tuned radio, bird bones hopping under his soaked parka. *explosives, kilometres* February wind in her sleeves, her tights. If only he would straighten his shoulders. *remote control, gun emplacements, 500 rounds of 6-inch projectiles* Soldiers with feeble artillery, lack of supplies. The day officially wasted, double homework, a forged note. She shushes him, and he kisses as if her tongue is a popsicle, his odour, musty towel and fir trees. Her sand-scraped Mary Janes clear a patch to kneel. It's this or a bus to algebra, grey horses back in her brain. She pretends she's one of his soldiers, his babble gunfire, takes aim at spotlit water dazzling with regret.

He shoots me outside the derelict movie house
—black trench, black boots, my broadsheet
newspaper headline, *Condemned*, a life

sentence of adolescence. Both of us too much,
rows of shark's teeth, Vishnu's arms, a crowd
of cow stomachs. He comes out in a hospital bed

after too many pills, a glossy flyer for a shirtless
boys night. I make him sweat the telling, my snapshots
limited to two dimensions. At MOMA, my shutter

freezes his back slouched beside a painting,
T-shirt blazed with a bright yellow *OOF*, the sound
of taking one in the belly. Who can deny

perfect exposure? I do. And we fight on a subway
platform, arms flapping, baring our rows of teeth.
His underground club versus my sleeping bags

scootched on a dirty floor. He takes the express
to the city; I snivel on the slow train to Queens
where the floor is hard, petty, and all my stomachs

hurt. I am still too much. He is gallery poise
face to the high-key light, dancing through
an anemone of muscled arms, ready for capture.

DOGS

We drank wine from scuffed
glasses in that stinking club

and bet we could seduce
the same woman. Your chair

sniffed hers, wet nose
to the question of her ear.

You, so eager, slobbered
flattery, brow a startled ridge

when the burr of my teeth
chafed your collar.

In the parking lot you declared:
I'm half in love, as if

that was obedience, your laugh
part yowl, part bark. I curled

in my seat while the engine
revved. Parked outside

my parents' house, you panted
cloudy drool into my mouth,

leg shaking the brake pedal,
flashing our signal. I sniffed

the seat belt's flat buckle,
waited for you to wake

from your dream of chasing
a bird around a lake.

She wishes they spoke as couples
spoke in films, half glances of devotion,
jokes by a lake with a tumbler of wine.
She writes sermons, and he jangles

a constant exit, keys in his anorak,
errands, chores, silence like grime
underfoot, muck in the kitchen corners.
Perhaps if she shared her worries:

Mormonism's white sheet snapping
the Americas, the leather Quran,
perfumed with tobacco, stuffed
in their mailbox. She could confess

that when the doctor blamed her uterus
for their lack of a child, she hid the news
so their pointless Wednesday churning
might continue. She could describe

pregnant brides, one so sick, she vomited
into a bridesmaid's bouquet, or the groom
who remarried while his first wife died
in hospice, or the couples who bickered

their vows. This is marriage, she wants
to shout, this broken, stumbling thing.
She'll tell him she cries after evensong,
dizzying ruptures that leave her

parched. And a fine, flinty lust rises
at the sight of her underthings dangling
from a doorknob. She will not tell him
she has imagined knifing her throat,

cupping the wound to feel life beat away,
or that once, she gave a woman a lift
home from town, and the woman bared
her breasts. All afternoon, she felt blessed.

She wants to tell him, when they first
met beside the chapel bake sale's frosted
cakes, she wasn't put off by his lofty
posture, his guileless eyes.

She imagined him ripe and yielding,
a fruit to peel and gouge each night
until there was only the pit of him,
hard and tasting of almonds.

turns up when I'm day drunk and half done waxing. I keep the chain on.

He cries. Shaved head, tricky eyes: one a mine shaft, one a lake.

Can his brother spare some T-shirts, can I run him to the bank?

I washcloth my armpits, rip the last strips of wax. He waits in the cedars.

We park where we parked as kids, a road scarred into a hill, baby seat
behind us, a crumby little judge.

He tokes and talks. *All those fucked-up pricks on Facebook with their wives
and dogs,*

unbuttons my skirt, works his bitten fingers in, squints against smoke,
still jawing.

When it's done, he sniffles, turns on the radio. *What it's like being married
to my brother?* then he yells for me to drive.

My card is finicky, three hundred a day. *Not enough for what I just did.
You got fat and all.*

I stare at my unwashed wagon, blossom sludge in the rims.

Anyway, I thought you were going to law school?

My husband will panic to find the nanny damp from swimming,
pound the redial like he's working on bail.

My card would buy a handful of days, stagger to the next party,
sleep out in the park,

hitchhike home different, more grateful, a thicker chain on the door.

Clay asks a guy in overalls the time then lopes into traffic, looking
only right,

not caring what hits him. The past spools slack. A buzzer rings.

High school doors swing out a hooligan crowd and he dissolves.

My legs, still raw from tearing those strips, goosefleshed, shimmying.

LETTER OF LAST INSTRUCTION

Our hatchbacks rattle home to husbands on Grindr
and siblings flimflamming for a loan and a lift to rehab.

We resuscitate parents, suction throat tubes, hot-wire
ventilators, change shitty diapers, then side-hustle,

craft exquisite communiqué at fifty cents a word for
Nigerian email scammers. While memorizing the sudden

death clauses of insurance policies, we short-order cook
for children, finish their homework, then slouch down

to basements of hydroponic funk and plastic sheathing
to tinker with our failed time machines, physics of regret

calibrated to a date of smoother thighs and our first
good review. We check that the ceiling beams hold

our weight, count razors and pills, lie clothed
in the bathtub with a toaster. We get stoned, scavenge

mouldy files to milk dead family and peevish lovers
for a tell-all, but find only rejection letters, unused

award speeches, college photos of best-selling friends
with thick hair and marketable teeth. We panic-read

student manuscripts, swallow genius like wet cement,
stomachs hardening. We send threats to our agents,

crude alphabets carved from newspapers and glossies
that no longer publish us. We douse our rants in cyanide,

dispatch them by carrier pigeon. In the longest hour
before dawn, we scribble—on windshields in lipstick,

on our office floors in piss, on bathroom walls in blood,
on paper, on paper. We pray the pigeons will come home.

Stoned on blueprint ink and Ritalin they mouth
concave, convex, titter over groin vaults and flying
buttresses, wrestle in sisal remnants behind the limestone

offcuts. Their porn is north light through vesselled
glass, rods penetrating earth, hand-rubbed
plaster, succulents, old growth ceilings vaulted

to Empyrean. They own geometry, sport an armour
of T-squares and bow compasses fringed in macchiato
foam. From coccyx to clavicle they're tattooed

in Fibonacci curls. They smoke Kiva in atriums,
specify Italian drywallers, six coats of Amish White
and the cheeky play of cirrus clouds in the master bath.

They angle pools to reflect only virtue, shape
vestibules of grace, cantilever mezzanines for peak
compassion, bestow the human constructible, the maze

arcade and rotunda of being alive. Beneath their gilded
transoms, frailty dissolves, that Carrara foyer with heated
inlaid walls more proud of you than your mother.

Fever on the streets as our planet swings closer
to the sun, as ocean levels rise, biohazard
atomizes, nuclear runoff seeps. Lives mundane

with disaster. At the store, we snipe over
which canned soup has more nutrition, chunky
or creamy, which shattered pack of crackers

has mice. A stock boy with peeling palms
counts water bottles, while outside, men
in lab coats debate timelines of extinction.

I climb into a shelf for the last box of oats,
and a woman in full makeup, French twist,
purse dangling from a charmed wrist, stretches

on tanned legs to help my husband reach
a can of waxed beans. Her fingers pulse
his biceps. His eyes finish her like a meal.

My T-shirt smells of dead guinea pig,
and I wish for one last bolt of catastrophe:
a fissure, a sinkhole in the dry goods aisle.

So that weeks from now, it will be my hair
unravelled, flecked with debris, my ash-smeared
skin in a strappy slip as I lie beside a naked man

whose name I do not ask. Too busy tracking
diseased dogs with my night scope and rifle,
too busy brewing carboys of anti-toxin,

wielding my flamethrower against mutant
spiders, too busy calculating orbit-altering
supernovas to settle for repopulating the earth.

1. Blowtorch, Acid or Plague.

You've abandoned high-minded ideals
of aging. Skin sags when it's afraid, a waist
grows lumpy with anxiety. The seismic boom
of immigration makes babies of everyone.
Are you even safe in bed?

1000-count percale machined by unskilled
children. Who knows what chemicals
they use to make things white. Your belly full
of Greek yogurt, floating on bespoke latex
foam and steady stock growth.

Security cameras assure you've made enough
to batten down. You watch news to seethe
over unmarked cargo ships and who's stealing
jobs, migrating to stain porcelain beaches,
the relentless shade.

Worse are the Chinese, you type, their termite
state chewing through phone lines, razing
craftsman homes. Hiding in the math
of your computer, edging in with sheer
numbers and shop signs you can't read.

On the playground, you once told a girl
with onyx pigtails, I'll be the queen,
you be the maid. Her eyes like blades.
Mother explained to the principal,
you meant, *maiden*; a little white lie.

2. At Fifteen You Fucked a Boy

Behind a shop, a smart-dressed boy from London
who winced at your laugh. You worried about getting
pregnant, your grandmother's swollen copy
of *Mandingo*, Papa the type to boil an uppity
boy in a vat. You think of him while googling

ways to tighten your neck, serums, remedies,
clicks that meander to faceless clove-skinned
men slick and hunched over blondes. Your fingers
tap-tap. Later, you look up websites where you
can donate to make a country great again.

3. What's Dark May Be Invisible.

A boy slips between the louvers. Bloody-faced,
a gun, a comb, car keys in hand. A hole
through his eye to reveal the stars. He was good
at history and physics; he coaxed plain girls
to dance. He looked darker in the sun

behind the shop, body loose like the life
he was meant to grow into. *Why do I even
appear to you?* he cries beside the custom
upholstered chair; shouldn't he grace his mother,
his sisters or the boys at temple?

You were the pretty thing who squealed,
slid hands under his shirt to feel a fine stranger,
the shyness of his chest caving and you claiming
each rib. Afternoon heat, clack of crated
bottles, your lips against

his neck, the spice of his mother's cooking,
all of it muddles in a misfire of your heirloom
synapses. The moon blinks through his hollowed
eye. What do they do to their skin, you wonder,
to make it seem so real?

Late to the wedding, bitches high-stepping,
that ruffled organza sashaying, tornado
hair, insect lashes, they crash the buffet,
jewelled acrylics dragging, cleavage full
of shrimp. They comandeer the bar to pour
thigh luges of French 75, butter the dance
floor, hoist the bride like a taffeta umbrella.

Swept up in a conga, he argues the merits
of Keynesian economics with a testy pink swan.
She proclaims him rich, pale, stale mediocrity
in retrograde, the anemic spawn of Thurston
and Lovey Howell. This bird: angora plumes,
diamanté incisors, barbelled tongue. He counts
fire exits as her spittle flecks his cheek.

Men pat their pockets. The swan flaps, pliés, tucks
his car keys under her wing. The first busboys tied
and blindfolded, first husbands shot. A waterfall
of crystal and china, tables cleared for wives
to recline in techno strobe. Bitches come armed
with an arsenal of dildos. Orgasms muffle the DJ
and the mewl of men crawling through blood.

His father foretold it with Ardbeg and a back slap:
Never bring a mouthy one home. Bridesmaids
rig rope for a groomsman piñata. While the bitches

twerk, he crouches behind a table barricade.
Wives in gowns stripped to the waist, shake
bottles of Dom, breasts juddering as they brine
the dead, then squat to gnaw meat from bone.

The danger is where we least expect it.

In the glue of the conference hall carpet.

In the tall woman's mouth.
The way her saliva infects

a stranger's heart, and he hangs off
her shoulder as she scans for doors.

Peril in law books, in the leading
and kerning. Some of us have stopped
believing in remedies,

she can't believe the man
is still talking.

Justice is chromosomal
Y marks the spot. Our part:

to be served, summoned,
gavelled, our existence
to cease and desist.

At dinner she latches on
with a group, and somehow
he's at her table for dessert.

Law keeps no language
for nuanced threat

for pained politeness
as the simplest way in.

                              At night our throats are sore
                              with fumes. Bodies slack, we foam
                              through muzzles.

In the morning a panel of revered
experts calls for transparency, clarity

and won't admit the story
they want ends with

                              a woman is so inconvenient,

that colour of lipstick,
a pall over the closing reception.

                              If it was really so bad, why didn't she
                              call the police? And if she did, well,
                              how rash and histrionic.

The keynote speaker insists,
there are no bad people in this field
just a few bad women.

The conference will investigate
low-VOC carpeting for next year.

                              Is it any wonder we all got sick?

CHRONIC

A tiny computer taped
to your chest records
a syncopated quake.
Miles away technicians
review your etchings.
Can they see what you see?
The past is a Morse code
of cataclysm, the algaed
harbour as you sink
below a freighter's keel,
thrash for surface, kick
back against his grasp.

Women who try to forget
decode worth in a cipher
of lists and likes, but a bad tide
is a bad tide. We are in waiting
rooms to report our own
drowning. We, who have
been perforated, remain
perforated. Esophagus, stomach,
duodenum, *Can you show me
where the pain is?* What gesture
do we use for decades,
for seaweed in our veins?

PRACTICE

Avoid intellectuals.
Choose accomplices
who know their hands:
surgeons, plumbers, art
restorers, a baker who
speaks only Portuguese.

Some will say
be yourself, but how far
has that gotten you?
Be the last milky
drips in the ice cream
carton, the satin lining
of a sable coat,
the merengue of a can
shaker at the paint store.

Seek out disaster:
robbery, earthquake,
hijacking, yard sale,
wherever the desperate
cluster skin to skin.
Make eye contact
as if holding a filament
in tweezers, smile
with the laziness
of a cat's furred mouth.

Map territory. Guest
rooms, loading docks,

parked cars, the shaded
grass between houses,
the countless sex dens
of shrubbery. Choose closest
and quickest; learn
to do things standing up.

Ready as you are, expect
resistance. The musky
tang of strangers
steeped with Sunday
service guilt, a cramp
in your calf, the need
to pass gas. Do not
be afraid. Stare through
the bay window of longing.
What is life if not respire,
palpate, salivate?

The "he" can be faceless,
nameless, guileless,
careless. Remember:
at the instant of your birth,
a girl's body passed through
the body of a woman.
Make your body
race. Raise your hips,
your eyes, exalt, exalt.
Cross the finish line
without looking
behind you.

Parisians prescribe ice baths for uncertainty.
Barometric pressure is the leading cause
of tears. Each time a doctor rubs her nose,
a bundle of bad news is born. Amniotic fluid
rises with the stock market. The butcher
uses a sharper knife for sinew than for bone.
Snails without their shells die of dread
before exposure. Miscarriage on Friday
means you still host Sunday brunch.
Fish can live on land if they'd just put
their minds to it. To morcellate your uterus
the surgeon will use a hand blender.
A seed germinates in a songbird's mouth
only if the bird stops singing.

LATE OCTOBER

He burns the hazard, blackberry brush.
Stamps a boot over smouldering slash,
incense of thorns, wine cinder.

The hounds are another matter, drooly chops,
hungry noses. They pace the grounds sniffing
for bone. We keep the house too cold

for children, fridge stacked with anchovies,
olives, gin. What do they eat? he asks. Flesh,
I say as I wiggle a broomstick past the flue

to dislodge a crumbling bird. Do children cry
over death? Do they cry over not being born?
He carves pumpkins with a slippery knife;

I follow to make sure he puts it away.
When he carries a bowl of pennies to the door,
I say, They've stopped that. It's dangerous.

He shakes his head, stymied by how much
we don't know. Dusk skulks in the grass.
Through fog they arrive by the gate, small

monsters, animals, aliens. They teeter and sing.
At the door, all growls, their tiny hands wither us.
And we wish we could give everything away.

IOWA

Days before your brother Paul
ends his life of wanting
behind a rooming house door,
you and I drive from Iowa City.
Tornadoes brew on the plain,
a week before cicadas rise
the world is not yet biblical,
and your brother, artist and con
artist, abandons gravity, loosens
his soil-bound self, leaves you
a voice message, exuberant
sizzle in his veins. Oh future,
to feel so wonderful. Inch by inch
our car crawls from thunderheads;
the highway offers us to open sky.
Air burns his unfinished skin,
for weeks, his body hidden,
unclaimed. We wait at the overpass,
a shadowy sliver of refuge where
two concrete wings clap together.

Technicians in lab coats predict
our family's extinction. Squatters
in the uterus grow fat on estrogen
and wasted space; a skeptical chamber
tips away. What did Darwin know
that we don't? What chromosomal
frailty backtracks here? Birds with two
beaks. Monkeys without tails.

Fortunes told, we are free to risk,
eat out-of-date seafood, careen
without seat belts. We swim
immediately after dinner, wash
pension money at the blackjack table,
open umbrellas indoors. We dress
the dog in foot pyjamas and smooth
his worried brow. We turn out

cupboards, tip drawers, roll rotting
logs, scrabble to rocks and wait
the night where the sea leaves life
in pools, certain we've lost something.
We try the 7-Eleven, the skate park, troll
gum-cracking girls and hooded boys
on dirt bikes for your father's eyes,
my mother's one turn of phrase.

Retired, we comb the earth's
edges, ice floes, cliffs, jungles, dunes.
Settle in a mud-slung hut, stooped
and shaggy-backed. We rise at dawn,
groom each other, then clutch sticks
to scrape small figures into walls,
chitter our private monkey language,
slap palms to ground and howl.

BIRTHDAY TOAST

Is there any sense in what washes away?
Husband and child, the rinse of divorce,
last threads of patience, our joints' spongy
tissue, our savings, our schemes.

Just for today, admit it's hard how we die.
We plod. Decay doesn't ask to be watched.
The years slacken our shape, stretch us
indistinct. Once, I looked at you and saw

the nerve of every age you'd been, a nest
of rough dolls. Were we ever young?
Not these hand-me-down scowls, exhausted,
fat and stiff, doll selves shrouded in cloudy

shellac. I've locked my keys in the trunk
of my car, left the sliding glass door ajar.
Cat's gone. Call it age when I turn on
the gas and forget the pilot's unlit.

No matter how we wax and dye, constrict
with Botox, Pilates or Spanx, no matter
how we antioxidize, the elevator doors
are closing, discarding us in a dim hall,

while cables rattle and ferry away
that panel of bright numbered buttons,
the ones we dared and didn't dare push,
so sure there would be more time. No rush.

WHAT WE MIGHT HAVE KNOWN

That we would be inspected, butcher cuts
on back seats, boys prying the edges
of our cling wrap, eager to pound us
tender, our Styrofoam trays cracking.

That we would be sampled in public,
squeezed, sniffed, weighed on rigged scales,
trimmed and trussed until we bruised
and blistered, until we bloated, past due.

That we would be suckled, slurped, bitten.
That, marinated in vomit, we would roast
on mattresses beside slivers of fevered
young, their arms strung around the fat of us.

That we would slouch bald in oxygen tents,
tubes draining our pink juices into plastic
sacks, chapped lips mumbling instructions
for the microwave and garbage day.

That we would be stripped for parts, gelatine
corneas, lung cutlets, offal trifecta: liver
pancreas, kidneys, our best holiday recipes,
the pristine, unused chambers of our hearts.

The time: exigent and precise,
10:17 or 2:42 with no one allowed in
early or late. A statutory holiday
so everyone has to cancel
vacation plans. Crazy weather,
hoar frost and summer snow
evaporating to thirty-degree parch.
A church in a neighbourhood
of cul-de-sacs, Bainbridge Crescent,
Bainbridge Drive, Bainbridge Gate,
Bainbridge Court, and a card
that reads: please arrive
on time to 2424 Bainbridge.
Road works blocking every entrance.
A florist who delivers wedding flowers
by mistake. A friend to slip
the bridal bouquet into my hands.
A friend to toss the bouquet.
A friend brave enough to catch it.
That all my ex-husbands arrive
with thin, blond wives in white
heels and pink satin. A pastor
who calls me Linda and Sandy
and Tracy. A procession begun
with a New Age pan flute rendition
of Bob Seger's Old Time Rock and Roll.
A drunk uncle to lurch and upend
the coffin so I tumble out, legs
splayed, bra gaping, the friend

with the bouquet lobbing it
just then to break the tension.
Hymnals in German, kneelers sticky
with uncured varnish, the janitor
rolling his mop bucket
in the vestibule. At the end
of the service, a storm to open
the sky. So that those I love
must huddle and cling under eaves
in disbelief. Let them topple
like bottles, fall like lovers
into one another's arms. Let the rain
on their faces look nothing like tears.

The opening line of "What It Was Like" comes from Tracy K. Smith's "At Some Point, They'll Want to Know What It Was Like" (*Life on Mars,* Minneapolis, MN: Graywolf Press, 2011).

"Letter of Last Instruction" was written in response to Wendy Morton's "Bernie's Funeral."

I owe so much to the editors and journals who published earlier iterations of these poems:

Ploughshares: "Analysis"
The Adroit Journal: "Fame"
The Puritan: "What Are the Architects Doing?", "No Place for a Heart"
The Malahat Review: "Ends of the Earth", "Late October", "Failing Photography"
Contemporary Verse 2: "Appeal"
Arc Poetry Magazine: "Of Factual Interest"
The Fiddlehead: "In Salem", "Birthday Toast"
Event Magazine: "What We Might Have Known", "Alphas", "Four-Eyed Girls"
glitterMOB: "Night at the Horseshoe", "Girl with Bear", "What It Was Like", "Hen Night"
SubTerrain Magazine: "Husbandry", "Sexy Kids"
Occulum: "Wife at the End of the World"
Glassworks: "The Vicar"
Jet Fuel: "Covenant, Junior High"
Dunes Review: "Iowa"
Canthius: "Ms. Clairvoyant", "For the Next Person Who Asks"
Prism International: "Dogs"
Canadian Literature: "Letter of Last Instruction"

ACKNOWLEDGEMENTS

My deepest gratitude to:

My family in Canada and the UK, especially my mom, Nancy Chen, the strongest, most generous woman I know.

Dionne Brand for her guidance and wisdom, and to Kelly Joseph, Anita Chong and the entire M&S team for their kindness and support.

My Lying Bastards: Sally Breen, Dina Del Bucchia, Keri Korteling, Judy McFarlane, Denise Ryan, Carol Shaben and John Vigna. These poems wouldn't exist without you.

Laisha Rosnau, Jennica Harper and Marita Dachsel. Every woman should have a coven. Thank you for your draft reading, spells and healing powers.

Sheryda Warrener, my ebullient guide. Thank you for the light you shine.

The women who inspire me through daily example, Annabel Lyon, Linda Svendsen, Alix Ohlin and Alivia Maric.

This book is for John, who knew, long before I did, it would exist.

Nancy Lee is the author of *The Age* and *Dead Girls*. An assistant professor in creative writing at the University of British Columbia, she lives in Steveston, B.C., with her husband, the author John Vigna.